THE POCKET GUIDE TO

BOWHUNTING

WHITETAIL

DEER

A HUNTER'S QUICK REFERENCE BOOK

Monte Burch

Skyhorse Publishing

Skyhorse Publishing books may be purchased in bulk at special discounts for sales promotion, corporate gifts, fund-raising, or educational purposes. Special editions can also be created to specifications. For details, contact the Special Sales Department, Skyhorse Publishing, 307 West 36th Street, 11th Floor, New York, NY 10018 or info@skyhorsepublishing.com

Skyhorse® and Skyhorse Publishing® are registered trademarks of Skyhorse Publishing, Inc.®, a Delaware corporation.

Visit our website at www.skyhorsepublishing.com.

10 9 8 7 6 5 4 3 2 1

Library of Congress Cataloging-in-Publication Data is available on file.

Cover design by Brian Peterson
Cover illustration: Thinkstock

Print ISBN: 978-1-63450-449-2
Ebook ISBN: 978-1-63450-467-6

Printed in China

CONTENTS

Bowhunting whitetail deer is exciting, fun, and challenging. Any deer taken with a bow is a trophy.

Bowhunting for whitetails is one of the most exciting, challenging, and satisfying forms of sport hunting. Thanks to modern game management, increased enforcement of poaching problems, the adaptability of the amazing whitetail, and a growing respect and love for their favorite trophy by hunters, whitetail deer populations have literally exploded across much of the North American continent. Whitetail deer populations in some parts of the country are as high or higher than before the country was settled, almost to the point of becoming "pests" in many urban areas.

Because of these growing populations of whitetails, most states and provinces have special bow or primitive weapons whitetail seasons. Many of these are long seasons, allowing you to bowhunt a full three to four months out of the year.

Bowhunting whitetails also offers the opportunity to be in the woods during some of the most enjoyable periods of the year—fall through winter. Bowhunting whitetails is both challenging physically and contemplative mentally. It's quiet time, a chance to evaluate your place in life—time to "think" if you will—a precious commodity these days. Successful bowhunting also requires good woodsmanship. If you're going to consistently be a successful whitetail bowhunter you have to work at it. You have to learn the animal's habits, spend a great deal of time preparing for the hunt, and then a great deal of time hunting. But that's what makes the sport so appealing. It is all encompassing. The skills needed, however, can easily be learned even by a first timer.

You may wish to carry this book in your pocket and refer to it as necessary until you master the woodsmanship and archery skills needed to bow hunt one of America's greatest trophies: the whitetail deer. Good Luck!

The first requirement, of course, is a bow. Bows consist of longbows, recurve bows, compound bows, and even crossbows

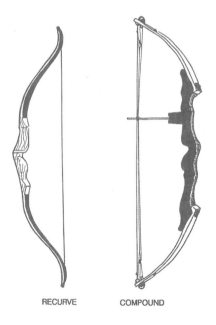

RECURVE   COMPOUND

Compound bows are the most popular type of bow now.

(where or when legal). My first deer was taken many years ago with a homemade Osage Orange bow. I then graduated to a Bear Kodiak recurve and eventually to a compound, and now due to age and a wrecked shoulder, a crossbow is my choice.

The choice of your bow often depends on whether you're just starting bowhunting or are upgrading. Bows are not cheap—you can easily spend $500 or more—but the only suggestion I can make is to purchase the best bow you can afford. In days past, bows were not quite as complicated nor varying in design, and it was usually a matter of picking out a bow at your local hardware or sporting goods store. These days you can purchase bows from big-box stores or online, but I would suggest buying from a reputable bow dealer who can also help you set it up properly. For the beginner, it's important to purchase a bow that's quiet and easy to pull and shoot. A bow with a higher brace height and less aggressive cam design provides a smoother and easier pull. Bow designs feature single, dual, and hybrid cams.

The bow for whitetail deer hunting has some requirements. First, it should be powerful enough to cause good arrow penetration. This means at least 45 to 50 pound draw weight for a recurve and can be 50 to 60 pound draw weight

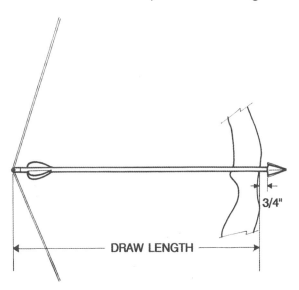

DRAW LENGTH

3/4"

for a compound bow. To provide the optimum speed and penetration, it's best to choose as heavy a draw weight as you can shoot comfortably and accurately. Not all bowhunters, however, have the same physical abilities or stature, and two common problems are incorrect draw length and too much draw weight. The draw weight can easily be adjusted to some degree, using an Allen wrench. Make sure you follow the bow manufacturer's instructions.

The bow should be matched to your draw length as well. This is the distance measured from the back side of the bowstring to the front side of the bow handle when you are at full draw. It is extremely important to know this for compound bows as the let-off will be different at different draw lengths. Most bow shops will be more than happy to match your bow to the weight needed as well as your specific draw length. You can, however, approximate your draw length by (1) pulling an overlong arrow to full draw and having someone mark the measurement on the arrow with a pencil, or (2) extend your arm out as if drawing a bow and measure from the front of your knuckles to the corner of your mouth with a yardstick. Naturally, your bow should be camouflaged, and today's modern bows feature the latest in camouflage.

You can kill a whitetail with a "bare-bones" bow. Most of today's hunters, however, add accessories to their bow to increase efficiency, accuracy, and comfort in shooting. Many of today's bows come in a "package" with accessories installed, including a sight, arrowrest, stabilizer, quiver, string suppressor, peep sight, and sling. If you purchase a bare bow, however, you'll have to install these accessories. You'll need a good hunting rest, one that allows you to draw the arrow quietly. You must also have a nocking point installed on your bowstring. This provides a method

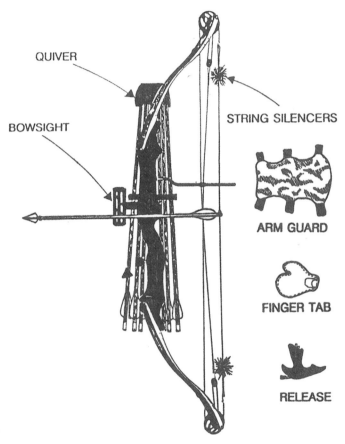

QUIVER

STRING SILENCERS

BOWSIGHT

ARM GUARD

FINGER TAB

RELEASE

of placing the arrow nock precisely in the same position each time. A nocking point can be installed at any bow shop or you can simply wrap the bowstring with tightly wound thread and cover with white glue. You can also install metal nocking points with special pliers, but they can slow down arrow speed. A bow square is

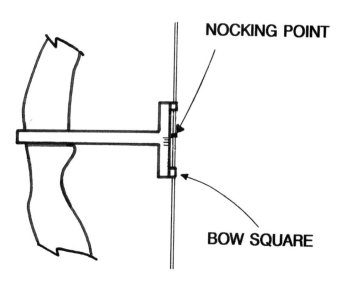

NOCKING POINT

BOW SQUARE

needed to determine the nocking point location. You'll also need string silencers and, if a compound, a stabilizer. You can also install your own sights, peep sights, quiver, and a kisser button, an accessory which attaches to the bowstring and helps obtain consistent anchoring points each time you draw. You may also need an armguard and finger tabs, if you're a traditionalist.

Many prefer a mechanical release these days, and a wide array of releases are available. These do, however, affect draw length. If using a release aid, some hunters add string loops, or a loop of string fastened to the bowstring behind the nocking point. The release is hooked to this instead of the string. These eliminate the problem of string wear by the release and also can add to consistency. They can, however, add a half inch or more to the draw length. An alternative is an eliminator button which locks the release in position and is easier to use in hunting situations.

Another piece of equipment you will probably wish to consider is a good bow case. A compound bow is both an expensive and highly technical piece of equipment and protecting it is extremely important.

Crossbows have become increasingly popular for deer hunting as more fish and game departments legalize their use. Regardless of some common thoughts, crossbows are not the same as guns in their accuracy, range, and abilities. Their disadvantages are their weight, awkwardness in the blind or on the stand, and they're still relegated to relatively short distances compared to rifles, shotguns, or blackpowder guns. Crossbows typically come in draw weights ranging from 130 to 165 pounds. The advantage they offer is you don't have to draw and hold the bow; simply point and pull the trigger. For those such as myself with age and two totally wrecked shoulders, they're the only bowhunting option.

With their popularity has come an increasing number of available models. They're not cheap, ranging from beginner crossbows at around $300 to crossbows costing $2,000. Most come in a package complete with light-gathering scope matched to the crossbow, quiver, and bolts or "arrows."

Crossbows have become increasingly popular, particularly among older hunters.

3. ARROWS

It's important to choose the correct arrows and broadheads as well. They should be matched to your setup. Using the correct arrow and broadhead for your bow and shooting can make a big difference in accuracy, speed, and even penetration. Earlier arrows were made of wood, but most of today's arrows are carbon or aluminum. Carbon is the best choice, but they're more expensive than aluminum. Carbon is faster and extremely durable. Carbon provides better penetration as it doesn't absorb energy, as does aluminum. Arrows, including carbon and aluminum, are available in various weights, depending on the wall thickness. If hunting bigger game, you may desire a heavier arrow. And, of course the arrow length must match your draw length. Arrow shaft length should be about ¾-inch longer than your draw length to prevent cutting your hand on the broadhead or bumping the bow facing.

Arrowheads or points are also available in a wide variety of shapes and sizes, including target, field, blunt, and hunting broadheads. You will need target or field points for target practice, and you may wish to keep an arrow with a field or Judo-style point for random shots at small game. Make sure the arrows, including points, are the same length, spine, or weight and have the same broadhead

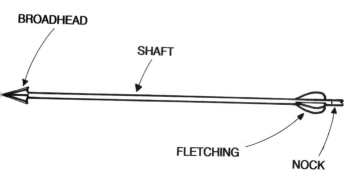

BROADHEAD

SHAFT

FLETCHING

NOCK

A wide range of broadheads is available.

weight. The correct broadhead is also extremely important, and there is a wide range of broadheads available.

Broadheads are available in either fixed or mechanical designs. Traditional broadheads are fixed and are still preferred by many bowhunters. Mechanical broadheads utilize hinges attached to swinging blades. In flight the blades are held secure against the body with a rubber O-ring. Upon impact the blades snap open. Mechanical blades offer the advantage of less wind planing than fixed blades, operating more like a field point in flight. They do provide somewhat reduced penetration due to the energy needed to open the blades. If you decide to utilize fixed blades, stay with the smaller diameter blades to reduce wind planing. Fixed blades may be solid or consist of inserts. The latter have small razor sharp be inserts that are fitted into a slotted point. They do not need resharpening as you can quickly change to new or sharper inserts.

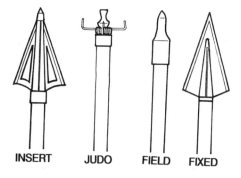

INSERT **JUDO** **FIELD** **FIXED**

The next decision is weight. The most common weights run from 75 to 125 grains, although there are lighter and heavier blades. The lighter weights provide more speed, the heavier weights more penetration. Matching the arrow weight to your bow weight is important. The formula used most often is six grains of arrow weight, including broadhead, for each pound of draw weight. Arrows in a variety of lengths and weights are readily available, or you can purchase the components and create your own arrows.

4. PRACTICE

As with most skills, shooting a bow is not really all that hard once you learn the basics. Developing proper shooting habits from the first is extremely important. I suggest you contact a local bow dealer, or join a local archery or bowhunting club if you're just beginning. The time spent with an expert will be well worth it. Then it just takes practice. If possible, practice a half hour or so a day. It is important not only to shoot from the ground in normal archery fashion, but also from elevated stands if you plan to hunt from a tree stand, and from different positions, like standing, kneeling, sitting, shooting left, and shooting right.

Practice, practice, and more practice is important for bowhunting.

Gadgets, gear and accessories are what makes bowhunting fun to some hunters. Some gadgets can increase the chances for success, as well as add to your comfort and safety.

CLOTHING

Clothing is probably the next biggest item and it's extremely important to choose the correct clothing not only to suit the weather conditions but also to increase your level of productivity. Quiet fabrics, such as wool and fleece, are better choices than hard and textured "loud" clothing. Make sure you have a wide variety of clothing so you can dress in layers to adapt to the changes through the day and season. Make sure any clothing you select fits properly and does not interfere with drawing and shooting your bow.

There is no dearth of camouflage clothing these days for bowhunters, regardless of the terrain, habitat, or weather conditions. Boots should match the situation, be comfortable, soft soled, and quiet to walk in, and of course camouflaged to match the situation. Many serious bowhunters prefer rubber boots that do not present scent over leather or cloth-style boots. Gloves, cap, and face masks complete the clothing selection. Camouflage face makeup can be chosen instead of a face mask, although the latter is better in early hunting season hunting when mosquitoes and gnats can be a problem. Other handy accessories include a pair of lightweight binoculars, safety harness for stand hunting, flashlight, day pack, knife, snakebite kit if early in the season, cushion for sitting, and compass and maps (or GPS).

A wide variety of gear is available to make bowhunting easier and more productive.

Although still hunting and stalking are exciting and productive methods of hunting whitetails, the single most effective tactic is to hunt from a treestand or blind. Both can be good in specific places and under different situations. Treestands are available in a wide variety of styles, sizes, and prices, including permanent, climbers, fixed position, ladder, and free-standing.

Treestands can be constructed permanently in place, or constructed and then fastened in place on trees, but they have several disadvantages. If permanently installed, they cannot be moved as needed to suit the changing seasons or deer herd patterns, and they can also damage trees. The biggest problem is safety. Constructed wooden stands eventually rot, or their components become loose and create a serious safety problem.

Climbing stands allow you to set up quickly in almost any location.

Climbing stands are extremely popular because they provide the ultimate in versatility. Find the deer, climb the tree, and hunt. When you're done hunting climb back down and take your stand with you. These stands are a must when hunting public lands. They are somewhat awkward and take a bit of strength and mobility to use. Climbing stands do have one disadvantage: the tree trunk must be fairly uniform in size, straight with no limbs, and small enough for the climbing apparatus to fit around. I tested the first climber, an old Baker, many years ago and they definitely changed bowhunting.

Fixed-position stands are fastened in place to the tree using a variety of means and are reached by strap-on ladder steps, screw-in steps, or blocks. These stands are the lightest in weight for backpacking, but are somewhat hard to use by the less agile.

Ladder stands feature a ladder with a platform on top. The stand is leaned

Fixed position stands are lightweight but require a method of climbing, such as the step stick shown.

Ladder stands are comfortable, but more permanent.

against a tree and fastened in place with a strap or chain. These stands have become increasingly popular for several reasons. First, they're comfortable, relatively easy to use by the less agile and older hunters, and these days they're available in two-person styles, an excellent means of introducing a youngster or friend to the pleasures of bowhunting whitetails. They are a bit heavy to tote around the woods and often awkward to put up. Many take two people to erect. But once in place their use is simple; just climb up the ladder and sit on a comfortable platform.

Also increasing in popularity are the free-standing or often called tripod stands because of the design of the support legs. These stands can be used in areas where trees are not available, such as shrub or brush country. They're comfortable to hunt from although fairly heavy to transport. One excellent use for them is positioned over a fence line or fence row with low brush rather than trees. Many tripod stands today also have manufactured blinds that can be installed on them, but most are primarily for gun hunters.

A number of accessories are available including strap-on or screw-in steps, hangers for your bow pack, and even video camera attachments. Special packs are also available for toting to the site.

TREE STAND SAFETY

Tree stands are dangerous, there is no other way to put it. Hunters are seriously injured or killed each year using tree stands, even experienced hunters. Regardless of what type of stand you're using, make sure you understand and follow all of the manufacturer's instructions for use and always use a good quality safety harness.

GROUND BLINDS

Ground blinds can also be used and are more comfortable to some hunters than

Fast, portable ground blinds have become increasingly popular.

clambering around a tree. Blinds can be nothing more than a few branches piled together to a more elaborate system utilizing aluminum, fiberglass, or wooden stakes and lightweight camouflage netting. A small stool gets you up off the ground for easier shots. These days a wide array of "pop-up" style ground blinds are available. They're lightweight, fast to set up, and are a great way to bowhunt. They're especially effective when bowhunting with youngsters or introducing others to the joys of bowhunting whitetails.

7. SCOUTING

Proper scouting is probably one of the most important ingredients in remaining consistently successful while whitetail bowhunting. You can't shoot deer unless you find them. You also can't shoot deer unless you know what they are going to be doing and where they are going to be when you want to hunt. This is called "patterning" and is the first order of business in bowhunting whitetails.

Start scouting well in advance of the season. If you don't already have a private area or favorite public area to hunt, contact the appropriate fish and game department and ask for their deer hunting information. Most offer pamphlets listing public hunting areas and information on harvest data, listing the previous year's harvest by county or area. Use this information to determine the best area.

The next step is to get a topographical map of the area. These are available at larger sporting goods stores and online as well. Study the maps to pinpoint the best possible hunting areas. Choose those that are more isolated, have natural travel lanes that funnel deer, such as hollows, saddles in ridge tops, or "edge" areas where rivers, creeks, ridges, fields, or a number of different habitat types come together. Aerial photos can also be a great helpmate including online info such as from Google Earth.

Then it's time to hit the woods. Most expert whitetail hunters scout year round. In fact, some of the best scouting information comes in late winter and many trophy buck hunters like to scout in the late summer months as well. The more legwork you do before the season begins, the better chances you'll have. As you scout, make a map of the area indicating all deer sign locations and noting the date and time. This information will become increasingly valuable as you hunt an area year after year. Locating, recognizing, and, most importantly, interpreting deer sign becomes easier the more you do it. Deer sign can be quite obvious or hard to find.

TRACKS

Tracks are the most obvious. Look for tracks around the edges of water holes, ponds, lakes, the edges of fields, and the soft earth in low areas of timber. One excellent place to find tracks and to start patterning deer is along a creek or small river that deer cross regularly. Common sense observation will indicate how old the tracks are if you have knowledge of the recent weather pattern. Tracks made before or after rain or snow are easily aged. Close observation of the area between the toes of a track in soft earth or mud will often indicate when it was made, to within a few hours. A sharp, knife-edge that is still damp usually

Tracks are the obvious deer sign—such as this big buck track.

indicates a fresh track while dried, crumbly material between the toes indicates an older track.

FRESH TRACKS

OLD TRACKS

Determining what made the track can also be easy or difficult. If there is only one set of tracks and they're big, the toes spread wide, and a set of dewclaw marks are behind the tracks, you're probably looking at those of a trophy buck. On the other hand, a large set of tracks intermixed with small tracks is probably a doe, or could be a young buck. It's almost impossible to determine 1- to 1½-year-old buck tracks from does.

Tracks may be made individually as deer feed, wander, and browse, or they may be condensed into trails with numerous sizes and types of tracks all in the same general area. Most trails also have the tracks headed in the same general direction, except for funnel trails which may have tracks leading to and from a feeding or bedding area. Locating deer trails can be frustrating in some parts of the country, especially in early bow season when trails are not as well established as they will be later in the season. Later in the season, as more and more animals use trails for specific feeding, bedding, and breeding areas, trails become easier to spot. Trails are a much more valuable sign than individual sets of tracks. Working into the sun early in the morning or late in the day with the sun at a low angle provides the best chance for spotting trails. Look for depressions made in the earth, disturbed leaves, or mashed down weeds and grass. Look for areas where more than one trail meets.

BEDS

One valuable sign is a bedding area. Beds are easy to find in the snow and grass, tough in rocky or sandy ground unless

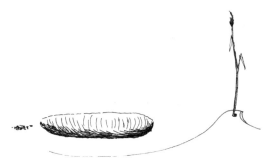

there is a deep layer of leaves. Beds show up as very slight depressions. When a deer rises from bed the first thing it does is defecate, and an even more positive sign of a bedding area is numerous piles of droppings. There may also be urination signs in soft earth or snow.

DROPPINGS

Droppings can, of course, indicate areas deer are using, but are most important when located near bedding areas. Deer droppings are small oblong pellets. Small round droppings may be rabbit. Close observations will indicate freshness and possibly when the animal used the area.

RUBS

Rubs or saplings with their bark peeled away by antler rubbing are probably the most famous deer sign. They do indicate a buck has been in the area, but only that.

Rubs, made by bucks rubbing their antlers against saplings, is another obvious deer sign.

Rubs may or may not be revisited. A single rub is useless as far as patterning bucks. A number of rubs, all in a line, however, indicate a line of travel and a possible buck trail.

SCRAPES

Scrapes or areas where earth has been pawed to bare soil are the most positive sign a buck has been using an area, but

Scrapes are deer communication signs made by bucks during the rutting period.

they can also be extremely frustrating and misleading. Some scrapes are made once and then never revisited, others are visited occasionally and some, the breeding scrapes, are used on a regular basis by does and bucks. The first step is locating scrapes and the next is determining their status.

Finding scrapes is easy if you know what to look for. Walking around the woods with your head down will usually result in nothing more than a pain in the neck. Instead, look for those areas where scrapes will most likely be found, then look for the scrapes. Regardless of where you're scouting, scrapes will be found in a relatively open area where bucks can see and be seen. This may be a clearing in the woods, even a small clearing, along an open field edge or an old logging road, an open spot next to a thicket, or a heavy cover area that may be a deer bedding area. There will almost

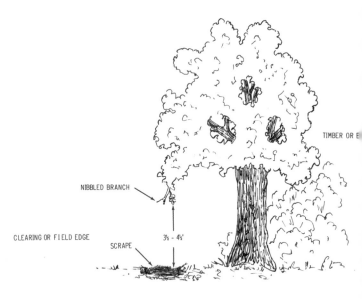

TIMBER OR E

NIBBLED BRANCH

CLEARING OR FIELD EDGE

SCRAPE

3½ - 4½'

always be a tree limb hanging 4 to 5 feet off the ground. If trees are not present, saplings may have scrapes made at their bases.

A nibbled and broken branch above the scrape is also a means of communication.

Scrapes are used by all the members of a herd.

Using trail cameras is a fun and productive method of scouting.

TRAIL CAMERAS

High tech has hit the deer-hunting scene in a big way with today's trail cameras. Well before the advent of even the primitive trail timers, I simply tied a black thread across trails to determine if and when they were being used, and in which direction. It worked, sometimes. Trail cameras make bowhunting for whitetails even more fun and productive. I use them to monitor trails first, then rubs, and finally scrapes. Seeing what's on the camera is almost as much fun as opening a Christmas package.

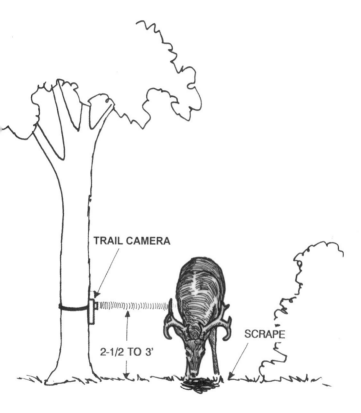

TRAIL CAMERA

2-1/2 TO 3'

SCRAPE

FOODS

Finding food is just as important as locating sign. Actually, it's easier to list what deer won't eat rather then what they will. They do, however, have preferred foods, and these will change as the food availability and seasons change. Browse, such as honeysuckle, is popular in the south, while acorns are the most common food in any

WHITE OAKS

locality they're found. We have a big apple orchard in our backyard, and it is full of deer in summer and fall until the white oaks start dropping their acorns in the nearby woods. Then the deer disappear. If you can find a patch of white oak acorns, forget everything else.

If agricultural crops are available, determine which are being used and then keep track of the changes in use as the crops are harvested or the deer herd changes their preference. Soybeans and alfalfa or clover are preferred early in the season while corn and winter wheat are preferred in the latter part of the season.

These days, food plots are very common and a great way of not only attracting deer, but providing enjoyment in land management for those who have the opportunity. White or ladino clover is the preferred food by many plot managers, but brassicas and winter wheat are also good choices. Food plots, however, do take work and equipment and can only be planted on private land with permission.

Numerous scouting trips should be made to determine the daily habits of the deer herd, and those habits will change as the foods and seasons change. Places deer frequent in late summer may not necessarily be the same ones they use in the winter. Using your map, compass or GPS and a log book, you can, however, pattern a deer herd.

Locating your stand in the proper spot is essential to whitetail bowhunting success. With proper scouting done, the next step is to determine stand locations. If possible, have several stand locations to adapt to changing weather and wind conditions, as well as to prevent overhunting a particular stand. Stands or blinds are best placed near water holes, field edges, ridge saddles, close to but not in thickets that may be bedding areas, and near major deer trails between areas deer frequent such as feeding and bedding areas. If at all possible try to locate near several such trails, or in a natural funneling area. Shown in the drawing are prime stand locations.

Some areas may be used only at night and others only during the mornings.

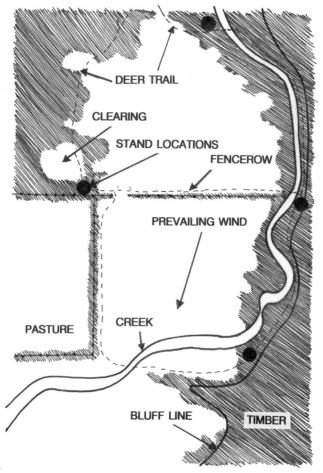

DEER TRAIL

CLEARING

STAND LOCATIONS

FENCEROW

PREVAILING WIND

PASTURE

CREEK

BLUFF LINE

TIMBER

Use trail cameras or daily scouting to determine when the area is being used.

Stands should be located downwind of the trails or area, according to the prevailing wind, but it is also necessary to have in mind additional stand sites overlooking the area for wind changes.

If possible, position your stand on the dark side of the tree or where there is some vegetation for concealment, but do cut away any limbs that might create shot placement problems. It's a good idea to try to fit your stand in place while scouting. Finding out your stand won't work with a selected tree in the dark of morning can be extremely frustrating. Height will depend on the terrain, from 12 feet above ground level for some ladder stands to as high as you dare climb with a climber.

Distance from the stand to the trail or shooting area should be what you're comfortable shooting. For some this may be 15 to 20 yards, although longer distance shooters may prefer greater distances.

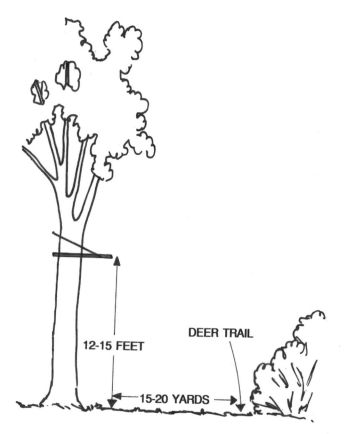

12-15 FEET

DEER TRAIL

15-20 YARDS

Remember, however, the height of the stand adds to the distance to the target. Once the stand is in place, get in it and do some stump shooting to make sure you have the range and angle estimated before the actual hunt. This is also a good time to clear away limbs or brush that may be in the way of shooting. Make sure, however, you have permission to do so, or that it is legal on public areas. If legal, mark the route to your stand using reflective trail markers for deep woods stand locations. Sure beats wandering around in the dark.

9. SCENTS

The single most important sense a whitetail has is smell. Sometimes deer will see or hear you but not become alarmed. One whiff of human scent, however, and they're gone. Regardless of all else it is extremely important to remember this when bowhunting, as you will have to be quite close to the animals to succeed.

The first step is to eliminate scent as much as possible. Bathe using an unscented soap and shampoo just before you hunt. Do not use spicy aftershave lotions or deodorants. Your clothing should also be fresh and clean, again washed with non-scented detergents. Do not eat spicy foods, nor spill aromatic materials, such as gasoline, on your clothing. Rubber-soled, or better yet, rubber boots that do not breathe are used by many serious hunters to prevent their scent from being dispersed as they walk to their stand.

The next step is to use a cover-up scent; however, these can easily be overused. One simple trick I've used for years is to store hunting clothes in a plastic bag with materials natural to the area, such as cedar, spruce, or pine

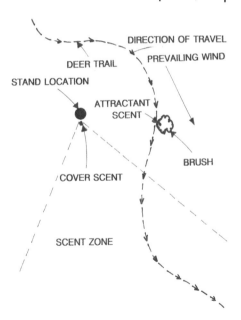

DIRECTION OF TRAVEL

PREVAILING WIND

DEER TRAIL

STAND LOCATION

ATTRACTANT SCENT

BRUSH

COVER SCENT

SCENT ZONE

boughs. Manufactured cover scents can be used but should always match the natural scents of the area.

Attractant food scents can also be used. Sex scents can be used just prior to, during, and after the rut, and include trail and scrape scents. These should not be used on our body or clothing, but should be placed near your stand at the location you wish to draw the deer to, or position a deer for a good shot. These scents can be easily overused.

Both calling and rattling can help produce deer for the whitetail bowhunter. Both, however, can also be overdone quite easily. Various forms of calling can be used throughout the hunting season. Rattling can be used throughout the breeding season, but is most effective just prior to the rut. Calling and rattling will work in any part of the country and the results can be fun and interesting.

CALLING

Calling consists of using three different types of sounds, the grunt, snort, and bleat, although there are many variations of these sounds that can be used. Calling can be done by mouth, or more easily with any of the many manufactured calls on the market these days.

The bleat is an attractant call that is most effective early in the season when does may still have young with them. It will attract does, and often bucks will also come to the sound out of curiosity. During the rut, does will come to the call and bucks will quite often follow.

The snort can be either an alarm communication, usually given by does, or an aggressive, dominant/submissive communication given by bucks. It is most often used as an alarm sound. It can, however, be given in answer to a snort given by other deer and will sometimes make them stop running and snort back. They may even come back to you.

The grunt is given by both bucks and does and has several forms, including a non-aggressive communication and an aggressive form used by bucks tending does in heat. The grunt is probably the widest used deer call and the most consistently effective throughout the season. It can, however, be easily overused.

Rattling is an easily learned and effective method of bringing bucks in—SOMETIMES! Authentic antlers, synthetic antlers, or a variety of rattling devices can be used. The latter are the easiest to carry and use. The tactic is simple: recreate the sounds made by bucks as they either spar or do battle. Start slow and softly, then increase the intensity and ferocity of the battle.

Bowhunting whitetails requires attention to detail and lots of patience. Following are some additional tips to help you score on your deer.

1. Approach your stand quietly and slowly from a downwind or cross-wind direction.
2. Don't cross game trails or walk to your stand from a direction deer will see you.
3. Take all precautions to ensure you don't disturb your hunting area any more than necessary.
4. While in your stand, move as little as possible. Use your eyes, ears, and nose, as well as the actions of animals around you to help detect deer.

An arrows kills primarily by causing blood loss or hemorrhaging. A gunshot can kill by hemorrhaging, but it also kills by the shock of the bullet, slug, or pellets.

It is extremely important for the broadhead of the arrow to strike a vital target area of a whitetail to ensure a quick, clean kill. This is basically the heart and lungs, although a hit in the major blood arteries or the spine can be effective. Even a paunch shot will bring down a deer, but is to be avoided at all times because the animal may take some time to die, usually resulting in a difficult tracking job. Although the hunting situation rarely offers the ideal broadside target, it is best with the animal standing broadside, looking in another direction or slightly quartering away from the shooter.

This position offers a shot at all the vitals. The target is just behind the point of the front shoulder. Remember, however, not to shoot too far forward as the shoulder bone can stop an arrow. Too far back and you risk a paunch shot. The target area is fairly small.

If hunting from a treestand, remember to take into effect the downward angle

IDEAL ARROW PLACEMENT

of the arrow flight. At long ranges you will almost invariably shoot under the target. If the shooting angle is almost straight down, as sometimes happens with treestands, aim directly for the spine. You'll either break the spine or hit the lungs. A chest-on shot is not quite as good as you must penetrate brisket and chest bones, although a high shot can cut the large artery in the neck. Probably the two worst shots are the quartering on and the directly away shot. In the quartering on shot, the majority of the vitals are protected by bones, while the paunch and bones from a rear-on shot can also act as an arrow stopper before the broadhead hits anything vital.

Very rarely will you have the best shots, but it is of utmost importance for the bowhunter to be patient and pick the single best shot offered. In some instances you will simply have to allow the animal to walk away. This is where proper stand placement, use of attractant scents, and calls to stop a deer and other tactics are important.

13. TRAILING

Once the arrow leaves the bow, the biggest chore of bowhunting begins. Rarely does a bow shot deer drop immediately. At the shot, carefully watch the flight of the arrow and the route of the deer. Listen carefully to the sounds made by the deer's flight. Mentally take note of the last place the deer was seen and/or heard. Don't, however, jump down and leave your stand to chase after the animal, unless you see the deer go down. Wait at least 30 minutes unless it's dark, raining hard, or snowing. If you push too fast, you may jump the animal and it may run again, even though wounded badly. While in your stand look for the arrow. If you see it, use your binoculars to examine it for any signs of blood. If you see no blood and are fairly sure of a miss, get down and start looking the area over carefully for blood.

If the arrow has blood on it, examine for the type. The color of blood and other matter found on the arrow indicates the type of hit.

If the arrow is not in plain sight, the first and foremost step is to look for it. If you can't find it, the next step is to look for the sign of first blood. This should be directly opposite where the animal was standing when you made the hit. Again, even if the arrow is missing, the type of blood as well as other materials, such as hair, stomach particles, and so forth, can indicate the type of hit you made. Play detective at this stage, do not get in a hurry.

One thing that's a must for trailing is toilet tissue. Tear off a small piece and stick at eye level on a branch or bush near the first blood found. Then look for the next spot. If you're lucky, you'll find a blood trail, but you may only find the tiniest of spots. Above all else, don't give up. If you can't easily find another spot, flag the last blood with two pieces

Success, and you're headed home with your venison.

of tissue and then begin a slow, ever-widening circle around the area until you find the next spot. Flag it and move on. If a deer bounds or stops, blood will be quite evident, but a slow walk may cause the deer to lose little or no blood for some distance. The toilet tissue trail at eye level will give you an indication of the general direction of travel, although deer will often circle. Forget about all those old sayings of where deer will go when injured and instead concentrate on locating sign.

Fresh tracks can also be a good indicator, and if in brush country, look for blood on the brush at body level as well as on the ground. If trailing at night, a camp lantern or bright spotlight can be your best aid in spotting blood trails, but make sure you know the rules and regulations concerning night trailing with a light. If you lose the trail, mark it well and continue the next day. It is of the utmost importance to find the animal or exhaust all efforts in determining if it has died or not.

Blood Trail Description	Location
Light to pinkish red, with foam or bubbles.	Lungs
Moderate red, with occasional bubbles.	Chest cavity
Bright red, in large amounts.	Heart, and main artery
Dark red to brownish coloration.	Liver
Dark red, with food particles.	Stomach

Follow all safety rules, including not climbing into your stand holding your bow. Instead, use a rope to pull your bow up into the stand.

1. Do not walk with an arrow nocked, as you can trip and injure yourself.

2. Do not climb into a tree carrying or holding your bow and arrows. Instead, get into your treestand and then, when safely belted in place, pull up your bow.

3. Make sure your equipment is in good shape, don't allow your arrow heads to contact your bowstring, and ensure all arrows and bow match.

4. Always use a safety belt or harness with a treestand or when climbing into or from it.

5. Handle your archery equipment with the same care as a firearm.

6. Positively identify your target before shooting.

7. Know what's behind your target.

8. Know where other hunters are in your area.

9. Always locate any arrow you shoot in the woods. Even if you don't hit a deer with it, another animal or person could be injured by it.

10. Do not hunt in trees during electrical storms or high winds.

11. Inspect treestands and make sure they are in good working order before using.

12. Know how to properly use your treestands.

13. Do not use treestands on slick-barked, dead, rotten, or otherwise dangerous trees.

14. Read your treestand's instructions and make sure you understand them.

VENISON STROGANOFF

Cut one pound venison round steak into ½-inch by 2-inch strips (approximately), removing all fat, sinew, and membrane. Salt and pepper the meat and dredge in flour. Brown the meat in a skillet in as little oil as possible. Remove the cooked pieces and drain on paper towels. Clean the skillet if needed. Return the meat to the skillet and add one package of dry onion soup mix, two cups water, and fresh or canned sliced mushrooms. Simmer until the meat is thoroughly cooked. Stir in one can cream of mushroom soup and, just before serving, stir in four ounces sour cream. Serve over noodles.

MORGAN'S VENISON LOIN

Our nephew Morgan's favorite method of cooking venison loin is to slice and pound the loin into cutlets. Shake Montreal Steak Seasoning on both sides of the cutlets and pan fry in a lightly oiled skillet. Cutlets are ready to eat in just a few minutes and are delicious.

GRILLED VENISON LOIN STEAKS

Our favorite loin recipe is to cut a loin into 1-inch steaks and marinate the steaks in a teriyaki marinade an hour or so before grilling. Grill over extremely hot coals, about three minutes to a side. Do not overcook. Serve with grilled vegetables (whatever is in season).

VENISON FAJITAS

We always grill enough venison steaks for two meals. The following night we have venison fajitas made with the leftover grilled loin and vegetables. Slice the steak into strips and cut any leftover vegetables as needed. Heat in a skillet with a package of fajita seasoning, following package directions. Serve in warm flour or corn tortillas. Note: If you have no leftover grilled vegetables, slice into strips the vegetables of your choice and cook them in the skillet first, before adding the cooked meat. Serve the fajitas with toppings of your choice: shredded cheese, salsa, diced tomatoes, shredded lettuce.

STUFFED PEPPER BOATS

Brown one pound ground venison with one large diced onion. Add a little olive oil as needed. Salt and pepper to taste and add ½ teaspoon garlic powder. When the meat is thoroughly cooked, stir in two cans diced tomatoes (for a spicier version, use part or all of the tomatoes and green chilies). Also add one can whole kernel corn with liquid. Cook this together for a few minutes, then add instant rice to the simmering pot. Cook over low heat until the rice has absorbed all liquid. Meanwhile prepare the sweet peppers by removing the core and cutting lengthwise into boats. Place the peppers into a baking dish and stuff with the venison filling. Bake in the oven until the peppers are tender, adding shredded cheese to the top in the last few minutes of baking. Serve with a baked sweet potato.

VENISON LIVER AND ONIONS

A deer camp favorite, this one is also easy to do. Slice liver into ¼-inch-thick slices and dredge in seasoned flour. Brown liver on both sides in a cast iron skillet in two tablespoons oil. Cover the browned liver with ¼-inch-thick slices of onion, then add a package of dried onion soup mix and cover with water. Cover the skillet and cook on low until the liver is tender and onions cooked. Serve with mashed potatoes.

VENISON CHILI

This is one of our winter favorites. Brown one pound ground venison in a tablespoon of olive oil in a four-quart saucepan. Add one large diced onion and one diced green pepper. Salt and pepper the meat to taste then stir in one package of chili seasoning (your choice). Add two cans diced tomatoes (or two cans diced tomatoes with green chilies) and two cans chili beans. Cook over low heat to desired consistency and adjust seasonings as needed.

Monte Burch (left) and nephew Morgan Burch.

Monte Burch has been a bowhunter since well before the advent of compound bows and resides on a farm in the

Missouri Ozarks, managed for deer and other wildlife. An award-winning outdoor photographer with numerous outdoor magazine covers, he has been a regular contributor to major national magazines for many years, with thousands of outdoor articles and over seventy published books.

NOTES

NOTES

NOTES

NOTES

NOTES

NOTES

NOTES

NOTES

NOTES

NOTES

NOTES

NOTES

NOTES

NOTES

NOTES